The Internal Journey of Us: Volume 1

Chazz Equanimity

ISBN: 978-0692228647 (IAMCZ Publishing)
ISBN-13: 0692228640

DEDICATION

This book exists for each of us. It is the unconditional, unfiltered, pure expression of life through our life. Internally we all journey, internally we all feel and experience the myriad of emotions, and internally we all have desires. What is shared here is for you. This book is not just the structuring of words and sentences, but the pure, honest reflection of you.. just as you are. I invite you to see your life through mine, I invite you to explore my life through yours, and I genuinely ask that you allow the opportunity for my soul and your soul to take this journey internally together.

CONTENTS

ACKNOWLEDGMENTS

I would like to thank everyone and everything, for making this possible. What is truly "good", has no foundation or relation to hurt. What is truly pure, has no need or existence in what is tainted. So with a humble heart, for all things, I say thank you.. for everything.

PERSONAL ENTRY #1 - 12:07AM
LOVE, YOU, AND LIFE

Nothing ever seemed so clear to me. It took for me to be totally alone to discover what is required from me to Love while with you. Love, being totally selfless in nature, must be my gift to you. Peace, being unrelated to conflict, must be the way in which I exist with you. These are just two of the fundamental gems that only the serious heart can discover. Maturity has blessed me with discernment at this stage in my life. A single man I am, but not lonely at all. Just alone peacefully, respectfully and maturely for the whole of humanity. I live without the desire of selfishness. What I do in my life is for you, because I understand deeply that there is no me without you. Every day I live to improve life for you. Every day I put my best foot forward for you. I don't seek anything in return from you, and I never will. As expectation has no place in genuine matters. And this matter of genuine compassion is what I live with, every moment of my life. Gratitude provides me with the opportunity to appreciate the truth of you. Making your imperfections beautiful. Making your growth an experience worth living for. I say these things to say that I finally understand what it means to Love you, truly Love you. So with everything within me, I will spend the rest of my life "showing" you that I Love you.

PERSONAL ENTRY #2 - 4:55AM
THE BEAUTY OF SELF LOVE

Learning to Love yourself brings life to you. Loving yourself brings security, true security. It comes with a quality of self-acceptance that cannot be disrupted. Once you truly Love yourself, esteem is dissolved. You no longer seek to measure/compare yourself to others. There is no longer a regard for self in terms of "high" or "low". There is only the sense of being present in the moment that carries importance. You understand deeply that you are uniquely "you". Not to be "trained" to be like someone else, and not to be "used" or exploited to hurt others. Life comes with a sense of newness within every moment when you Love yourself. Boredom dissolves, insecurity dissolves, all aspects of dependency dissolve. Love does not need reassurance. So when you truly Love yourself, expectation is also dissolved. You are only left with the full capacity of compassion within you. Hurt no longer has a place in your life, frustration is but a memory, and peace becomes the intent of every action in your life. This is what you deserve. This is the beauty that comes with Loving yourself, truly Loving yourself.

BEYONG THOUGHT ENTRY #1
PRIORITIES, RELATIONSHIPS: THE SIMPLE TRUTH OF IT ALL

Although sometimes it seems like everything is requiring your time and energy, you don't have to try to get everything all done at once. Just do things in the order of most important to least important, and it all works itself out. This is the simple truth to prioritizing. This is the simple truth to establishing order in your life. This is also the simple truth to maintaining unity in a relationship. When we see things honestly, without bias, but with peace as the premise, there is no regret in terms of our actions. However, this simple truth is rarely ever practiced in relationships. Instead of honesty without bias, many proceed with actions selfishly. When we pursue desire selfishly, the ability to prioritize becomes the need to satisfy that desire selfishly. Because relationships require unity, there can be no selfish action. There can be no attempt to place oneself above the other. So in terms of priority, and relational order, both parties must understand and address matters from most important, to least important "selflessly". When both parties see this simple truth, the relationship has order. Peace, respect, and Love are present. There are no arguments, only genuine discussions. There are no lies, only beautiful moments of truth. There are no attempts to control, only opportunities to explore life respectfully through freedom. And this compassionate gift of freedom, is what allows the relationship to grow beautifully, just as naturally as life flows through the both of you.

PERSONAL ENTRY #3 - 11:45AM
YOUR WORTH IS LOVE

Loving you is worth it. No aspect or variation of your life deserves to be without Love. This is something I'm sure of, just as I'm sure of the fact that Love must be the way I treat you. There is no "true" relationship without Love. There is no true sense of compassion without Love. Love must be the way in which we do "all" things together. I won't speak a word towards your existence unless Love is placed delicately yet firmly within my intent. I won't share any action with you unless Peace is the premise of my motive. As Love is peace, so must I be Loving "peacefully", for the pure existence of you, each and every day of my life.

PERSONAL ENTRY #4 - 2:06AM
RAIN

Rain, I find you beautifully truthful. You cannot be overlooked, you are critical to life. Nothing about you is destructive, instead you are purely refreshing when understood properly. Vital, yet artistic, you reshape landscapes with a uniqueness all your own. You bring new life through your nutrients. I need you, just as I need the sun, just as I need the Earth, just as I need food.. just as I need Love.

PERSONAL ENTRY #5 - 7:52PM
GENUINE REFLECTION OF LIFE

I want nothing from you, even as I offer you all that is genuine within me. I still want nothing from you. Not because I'm too good to take things from you, but because I value you far more than any expectation. You are not a commodity in my eyes, you are not disposable within my heart. You are sacred. You bring with you, life.. and that will forever be more than enough for me. Truly grateful for your existence I am, even before we meet. Thankful for your life I must be, because the gift of your life is what also brings life to me. There is a mirror that we both have the ability to share, and this mirror becomes "us" internally.. once Love is the reflection.

PERSONAL ENTRY #6 - 8:37PM
THEN CAME THE MIRROR

He never checked to see if she wanted to be with him. He never even thought to see if she had started liking someone else. He just Loved her anyway. She would do things in a disrespectful manner unknowingly to get attention. He would simply just respect her anyway. She even attempted to reach out to others for superficial comfort without sincerity. He just met her with genuine compassion anyway. Then came the mirror. She finally discovered what he was doing the whole time. He had told her a story before, that stated that a lady treated him the way he was now treating her. She then understood the beauty of his actions, despite her actions. She grew from this moment. Then later in life, she was approached by a man, doing the same things she used to do unknowingly. So this time, she never checked to see if he wanted to be with her. She never even thought to see if he had started liking someone else. She just Loved him anyway. He would do things in a disrespectful manner unknowingly to get attention. She would simply just respect him anyway. He even attempted to reach out to others for superficial comfort without sincerity. She just met him with genuine compassion anyway. The beauty of this, is that Love brings Love. Love is never responsible for hurt. Love then teaches Love, making Love possible within someone else. Love just has to be the mirror that we desire to see through.

PERSONAL ENTRY #7 - 4:36PM
WITHIN YOU

Inside of you is everything you will ever need in this life. Inside of you is the Love you seek. Inside of you lives the truth of you, the truth of life, the truth of humanity. What you truly need in life spiritually, does not exist outside of you, but within you. What is deeply vital to your emotional growth is already inside of you. What I'm speaking of is your genuine, unfiltered, unbiased, honesty towards self. Through self honesty, the lies dissolve, the emotional growth needed to Love unconditionally can be explored, and peace can be reunited with passion in the most beautiful of ways. You deserve to truly live a genuine life, all you have to do is be honest within yourself, about "everything", as peacefully as possible.

PERSONAL ENTRY #8 - 6:46PM
THE SOUL SHE DESERVES

I've decided not to speak to any potential woman I'm attracted to, in a way to "be" with her, unless I'm certain that I have my life in order. This was a decision I made many years ago. This was a decision I made once I understood that I must present to her nothing less than Love, at the “beginning”. Since that time, I've healed old wounds, I've dissolved any need or desire to judge. I've also removed emotional hurt totally from my life. Because when/if I meet her, I want to be certain that she understands that I've been living for her, the whole time.

PERSONAL ENTRY #9 - 11:05PM
MORE THAN LOOKS

What makes you beautiful to me is not your looks. It's not your hair texture or skin color. It's the way your heart responds to me. It's the way your soul kisses me. Never blinded by a woman's make-up and wardrobe will I ever be. While I can appreciate a woman with cultural or eclectic taste, when it comes to fashion, I'm much more concerned with the aspects of life that don't require peer approval. Uniqueness is a born gift we all carry, it's one that I would desire to share with you. It's one that would allow Love "in", for the rest of our days together. It's one that I hope we can both explore compassionately together.

PERSONAL ENTRY #10 - 7:06AM
THIS MORNING

Not every day I wake with the same feeling. While peace is the foundation that I wake with every morning, it can manifest itself in a myriad of ways. This morning, peace finds me in calm, yet subtle compassionate state. Gratitude seems to be moving through me, moving more towards the front of the emotional line within me as my senses awaken more and more this morning. To play with my imagination a bit, I would say that this would be a morning where (if I was with someone), I would kiss her as she sleeps. I would place my heart as close to hers as I could, and hope that my energy of thankfulness, gratitude, and appreciation for her existence in my life could somehow find it's way into her most current dream. Maybe one day this figment if my imagination will reach the actuality of true existence between her and I. But since the truth of my life (this morning) moves without that possibility of her, the energy of gratitude, compassion, and appreciation will surely find it's way into my actions toward others quite peacefully. As the beauty of what we feel genuinely inside of us is never wasted, when we accept the truth of where we are, just the way we are. This is the honesty of my life, that I see, feel, accept, and appreciate completely.. this morning.

PERSONAL ENTRY #11 - 10:08PM
TRUTH WITHIN BECOMES PEACE WITHIN

I don't live the lies we are taught anymore. I've decided to live without them totally. I've decided to live peacefully, and honestly within myself. To do so, I've also discovered that I must bring peace and honesty with me to you. So with peace as my premise, I won't provoke conflict ever, but I won't negate honesty ever either. This delicate balance of compassion, awareness, and empathy has led me to change the way I view, respond, and relate to other people. I now make sure that my actions are shared with a Loving quality, I no longer take things, remarks, or judgments personally. I simply live for you, even if you have yet to discover the beauty of living for me.

PERSONAL ENTRY #12 - 10:08PM
THE EXPRESSIONS OF TRUTH AND LOVE, THROUGH SELF

I'm finding it easier and easier to express myself. It feels good because I understand why it's becoming easier. It's because I do it all day long. Through self honesty, I've learned the art of self Love. A beautiful gift from yourself to yourself. There is nothing in life like it. There is nothing in life that offers you more vitality. To truly Love self, is to truly Love others, and when you truly Love self and others, you truly "live". The expressions I share daily, in my life these days, come with a deep sense of truth and compassion. Every chance I get, even if it's in the most subtle of ways, I do my best to share some aspect of Love with those I encounter. I do this by never separating myself from Love. This allows every action from my being to exist with Love's energy. As this is something I truly feel everyone deserves from me. And through the sincerity found in the honesty of my life and my intentions, I will continue to live this way for each of you, until my time on Earth expires.

PERSONAL ENTRY #13 - 5:56AM
SELF HONESTY IS THE BEST TEACHER

With there being no better teacher than self honesty, I have no choice but to improve greatly for myself, as well as for others, from the premise of this understanding. Most would say experience is the best teacher. But if that were true, then no one would argue, no one would fight, and there would be no wars. Because "experience" would have surely proven (through past experiences) that these methods don't bring peace at all, yet we continue with the same patterns anyway. Which means experience actually "teaches" us nothing at all fundamentally. The actual learning that many confuse with experience is the moment of honesty, where one looks internally and discovers wisdom in a given situation. It is this genuine quality of looking inward that I call self honesty. Self honesty does not happen when we make things up, or imagine, or assume things (based on what others have said). Self honesty is the unfiltered, peaceful, unconditioned approach to all information received through our senses. This approach must not be biased, must not come with the confines of experience, it must not come with a preconditioned "method", and it must not come with anything not "actually" known to be true. Self honesty removes frustration, as frustration is rooted in the denial of the fact of a given situation. Self honesty also removes hatred, because it enables us to see things as they actually are, without the need for selfishness. Self honesty dissolves all insecurities as well, because self honesty is the beginning of self Love.

PERSONAL ENTRY #14 - 12:55AM
LOVE'S UNDERSTANDINGS

Never forgetting what I've been through, but keeping it far enough from the present to ensure that I live every moment "in" the moment. Understanding what place memory has in my life, while appreciating the genuine beauty of attentiveness. These delicate, yet instrumental functions are learned through understanding what it truly means to Love. Realizing that arguments only happen when at least "two" selfish people are present, has led to me to not being in an argument for quite some time. Accepting my responsibility to myself, and to others respectfully and peacefully, is also a gift discovered once Love is understood. There is an aspect of intelligence that becomes very active within you when you Love. It comes with a deep sense of compassion for all life. I've been totally transformed by this ability to Love. The improvements in my life may appear to be gradual, but the initial change happens immediately. Because Love is understood within me, I'm now able to share genuine communication with others. I'm able to truly appreciate the truth of us all as human beings, and most of all, I'm able to add to the peace that you and the rest of this world so much deserves.

BEYOND THOUGHT ENTRY #2
JEALOUSY

Jealousy is a form of dependency. It exists as a survival mechanism in needy children. It is used in children to regain the attention of the person they depend on. Jealousy is also a form of control. When a person accepts this type of jealous relationship from someone, they immediately become confined to meeting the needs of the person that is jealous. The person that is jealous then has the ability to manipulate the other person. There is no Love in jealousy. There is no peace in jealousy. There is no freedom in jealousy. A relationship that involves jealousy is a relationship of emotional imprisonment. True happiness will never exist in such a relationship, only the needs for escapism and control. In relationships that involve jealousy, you have one that seeks to control, and one that seeks to escape the control. This leads to lies, abuse, emotional stress, and many other unnecessary dynamics of life relationally. As a child, jealousy has a function of survival, because as children, we are born dependent on someone else. However, as adults, jealousy becomes one of the major reasons relationships involve emotional hurt. As adults, there is no need for jealousy. As adults, one must not seek to control or manipulate others. As adults, one must become totally secure, to ensure that all functions of dependency are dissolved within them. Jealousy as a child can be understood, due to a child being needy of someone that provides a primary source of care. But as an adult, this must be something we totally grow out of. It's something we must totally dissolve within ourselves, if we are to ever truly Love someone. As the heart that carries jealousy, becomes the heart incapable of bringing Love.

PERSONAL ENTRY #15 - 11:53PM
ME FOR YOU

Within the existence of everything, there is you. Organically created from everything found in life, I feel you, I appreciate you, and I thank you. Minutes, hours, nor days will have a bearing on how I treat you. Instead, my heart, passion, and care for you will transcend lifetimes. With a genuine soul, I owe these gifts of attentiveness to you. With a pure heart, there is no way I could be your reflection without existing this way for you. Life has gifted me the opportunity to "be" here with you. So with Love, unconditionally, I'll meet you. I'll meet you the way the truth meets you. I will meet you the way peace meets you. I will meet you the way compassion meets you. With a freedom never to be compared, disrupted, or envied, I truly wish the best for you. To be totally honest, I must share that I Love for you. Not just today, but every day.. even before I meet you.

BEYOND THOUGHT ENTRY #3 ACCEPTING "NOW"

Even on the worst day, it could be worse. The idea of measuring or comparing one day to the next becomes the root of anxiety in itself. As there is no anxiety without the functions of imagination and comparison. This psychological "trick" we play on ourselves, creates stress that builds within us. The energy we start our days with can be stripped away mentally, due to this way of thinking. With thought comes beauty, when understood and used properly. But when thought is misunderstood, and used improperly, it creates immense stress and dysfunction in our lives. There is no peace, Love, or acceptance that exists when we use thought improperly. One improper use of thought occurs when we compare ourselves to others. Many people state that we should measure ourselves, not against anyone else, but against who we were yesterday. This too is incorrect. For one to truly accept self and live peacefully, requires that one do away with self measurement totally. Because as long as there is self measurement, there will exist the issues that come with self esteem, an image to uphold, the opportunity for emotional let downs, and no sense of true self acceptance, which in all cases, create dynamics in life associated with self hurt. For example, you can "remember" that you ran a mile in 6 minutes a year ago, but if it takes you 10 minutes to run a mile this year, don't see yourself as "less" than who you were last year. Instead, see it as information to truly accept who you are now "honestly", then, from the truth of you, proceed with the most appropriate course of action to grow as peacefully as possible. The same goes with a job, or an amount of money, or a lifestyle you once had. Never "compare" or "measure" yourself to who you were, just use it all as helpful information to truly "accept" who you are "now". As the beauty in life comes from the genuine acceptance of who you are, where you are, and how you are "now". The true beauties of life never come from the reviewing of the past or the projected desires one may have in the future. At times reviewing the past can bring a sense of accomplishment; just as a desire projected into the future, due to expectation, can bring a sense of excitement and vigor. But just as there is no true joy in accomplishment, there is equally no true joy in anything born of expectation. Because accomplishments only feed the ego and expectations are only thoughts we selfishly place on an unknown future, they have no true substance once selfishness is removed. The true feeling of joy happens only in that given moment of joy. The instant one is able to say "I feel joy", the true moment of joy has ended, and the remembering or recalling of the moment of joy has begun. This happens because all things that are truly sacred and beautiful in life, exist without the boundaries of time. This means that nothing with the beautiful quality of sacredness can exist in the past or the future. It can only exist in the present. Which means, if you are to truly feel and live Love, you must "be" present. Not in the past and not in the future of your life, but in the present. Present enough to truly accept and appreciate the truth of who you are, how you are, and where you are "now", unconditionally.

BEYOND THOUGHT ENTRY #4
THE BEAUTIFUL TRUTH OF OUR EMOTIONS

The relationship you have with yourself, becomes the relationship you share with others. If you are indecisive within yourself, when it comes time to do things, you will be indecisive with whomever you enter into a relationship with. The same is with honesty. If you are not honest with yourself, it will be impossible for you to be honest with another. This human truth, when understood, can remove all emotional hurt from ones life. Once we understand that the way we feel about others is actually the way we feel about ourselves, we can then work "truthfully" on dissolving the ways in which we hurt ourselves. Contrary to what others may say, the truth of emotional hurt is that it is totally our own doing. No one is truly capable of hurting us emotionally. When we hurt emotionally, it is our own doing because we "are" our emotions. Our emotions are triggered by what we like or dislike, what we value or don't value, and by what we've experienced or not experienced. Our emotions are not controlled by what someone else values, thinks, or goes through. Our emotions are called upon by us. For example, if someone you don't care at all about says "I never want to talk to you ever again", you may not have much of an emotional reaction in terms of care for that person. But if your wife or husband of 20 years, or your child said something like that without warning, your emotional state may be drastically different. They could both mean that statement the same exact way, but because "you" care more for your husband/wife/child more than the other person, it may affect your emotional state of being in a very different way. So when we say "you make me angry" or "you make me happy", we are actually making false statements. This is because happiness is determined by what "you" feel satisfies you, the same way anger is determined by what "you" feel upsets you. What satisfies you may be very different from what satisfies another. Just as what may upset you could be very different from what upsets another. So in terms of emotional understanding, one must truly understand that they are the source of the emotion. Then, once this truth is accepted, emotional security and emotional maturity become the foundation of all future actions in one's life.

PERSONAL ENTRY #16 – 11:01PM
COMPLETE

Nights are never lonely, or empty. Nights simply exist without you. They are full, even without you, because I'm complete within myself. There is room for you however, to be complete with me. But for you and I to both exist completely, you must be complete as well. Not lonely, or empty as you exist alone either. Because if there is an emptiness or loneliness that exists within you, then you will use me to fill that void. And where there is Love (Self Love), there is no void, only the fullness of each moment, as each moment. No expectation to be met, no desire that overrides the fact of a given moment, and no attempt to escape the feelings that exist in the moment. We both must be whole, if we are to truly be whole together. As I am whole "completely", for you.. right now.. at this moment.

PERSONAL ENTRY #17 – 8:27PM
IN THIS MOMENT

Remembering when life was easy as a kid. Thinking about the good ole times. Wishing for a different life. These are all things I have no room to entertain at this stage of my life. These memories don't affect my present anymore. I now live in the moment "daily". If it doesn't add to my life in the moment, I don't seek to purposefully remember it. If it doesn't bring clarity to a situation I may be facing, I don't attempt to recall it. For now, my life is right now, not in yesterday and not in tomorrow, but right now. The things I seek to do with my life require all of my energy to spill into what is currently happening. I have no room to waste the gift of thought and imagination in areas that don't improve life for you and I. Not right now, not in this moment, and as far as tomorrow is concerned, well.. I haven't put any thought into tomorrow..

PERSONAL ENTRY #18 – 12:14AM
EVERYTHING

I want to be everything with you. Not everything "for" you, but everything in a way to not limit you. Your life deserves freedom compassionately. Just as your life deserves Love unconditionally. So with a pure heart, I desire to exist with you freely. With everything being the genuine possibilities of your life. With everything representing the limitless nature in which I'll share my respects with you. With everything being all that is Love for you. This is why I want to "be" everything "with" you. To ensure that I take "nothing" away from you.

PERSONAL ENTRY #19 – 9:15PM
ONE DESIRE THAT STANDS OUT

If there is one desire that stands out to me in this moment, it's the desire to explore life honestly with you. To truly see what you see. To genuinely understand why you feel what you feel. I desire to explore lifetimes with you. Not for the purpose of recreation, but to truly discover what is sacred in life "with" you. I understand that True Love is sacred. I also understand that True Love requires honesty. So with Love and honesty, I desire to share my life with you.. and I desire to share my life "for" you.

PERSONAL ENTRY #20 – 2:57AM
MY LIFE, IS MY OFFER

Be naked with me. Not physically, but spiritually. Internally, meet me with your soul first. Allow Love, peace, and sincerity to explore us totally. Give freedom the chance to become us unconditionally. Give life a chance for us to add to it. Give me a chance to Love you. Give yourself a chance to truly be Loved. Because from me to you, I owe you the chance to be Loved, I owe you the gift of freedom unconditionally. I owe life the beautiful opportunity for us to be one. In other words, I owe your life the existence of mine.. peacefully, respectfully, and totally.

PERSONAL ENTRY #21 – 11:27AM
IT MUST BE MORE THAN SEX

Sex must not be the way we resolve any issue. Sex must not be used as a bargaining chip to gain favor in a particular situation. Sex must not be seen as a way to escape life. Sex must also not be viewed lustfully. So, in essence, sex must become more than sex. Sex must become so much more than just sex, to the point that it becomes disrespectful to even call it sex. Sex must be transformed into the most intimate aspect of freedom between us. So intimate that the two of us become one without the need for personal desires. Seamlessly connected spiritually we must be. So intimate that our lives blend beautifully. So intimate that without speaking, your soul sees the truth of me. This is why I say sex must not be the object of resolution, favor, escapism, or lust in our relationship. Because the moment sex becomes these things, we would no longer be sharing the intrinsic beauties that come from existing with joined hearts. Our souls would no longer be able to share a genuine connection with one another. And what was once pure between us would be no more, because at that moment, we would no longer be Loving.

PERSONAL ENTRY #22 – 11:35PM
VALUE

Without ever meeting you, I value you. Without knowing your name, your age, your gender, or your view on life.. I value you. This value that I feel for you comes from the understanding of life beautifully. Life, being extremely delicate, must be met with my spirit's intentions this way. The value you carry, to me, is a value beyond measure. A priceless value. One that cannot be compared, altered, removed, or overlooked. What I see in you is life. What I feel from you is life. So with my life, I'm willing to share the immeasurable with you.. unconditionally.

BEYOND THOUGHT #5
LOVE STARTS WITH SELF HONESTY

Love, being genuinely unconditional, requires freedom. Where there is no freedom, Love cannot exist. Therefore, for freedom to exist within self, honesty must be present totally. Self honesty allows us to truly see ourselves beyond condition. This freedom, from condition, gives us the capacity to explore ourselves beyond our experiences. This quality of honesty changes how we see the world in a deeply fundamental way. When we are totally honest within ourselves, innocence is restored. The pure quality of peace, through existence, becomes the way we desire to approach others. The movements of humility and compassion begin to order our emotions as we go through life. So many beautiful things "happen" as part of this transformation through honesty. Passion becomes "real" and pointed, in a genuinely creative way through honesty. Selfishness is dissolved through honesty. To discover true honesty though, one must be extremely serious internally. For example, one must be willing to remove every drop of self esteem, as esteem is not the "truth" of us at all, but instead, it's a condition that arises in the form of measurement due to insecurity. Through self esteem, we measure ourselves. This measuring of self is rooted in insecurity. When we are not insecure at all, we have no need or desire to measure ourselves. This trap of insecurity, through self esteem, has divided the world for thousands of years. Self esteem leaves us feeling "better" or "less" than another, or "just as good or bad" as another, depending on if it's "high" or "low" self esteem. (The quotations used in the previous sentence were to reference the way in which self esteem divides us through measurements.) This is why self esteem is the trap of insecurity that we must be able to see honestly. Because when one is insecure, one cannot Love, and when one cannot Love, one cannot be peaceful, and when one cannot be peaceful, one cannot truly be free of the enslavement of self hurt. Self honesty requires that we be capable of seeing the movements and traps of insecurity acutely, in a way to ensure the dissolving of it within our lives. Self honesty requires that we see ourselves, free from any and every form of measurement and control, as what is truly sacred in life exists beyond measurement and control. What is sacred is pure, what is pure, is honest, what is honest is freedom, what is free is peaceful, and what is peaceful is Loving. While, on the other hand, measurement is a form of judgment, and what is judged cannot be seen in a pure way at all, thus negating freedom, thus incapable of Love. Also, what is controlled is not free, and what is not free, cannot exist peacefully or purely, and what does not exist peacefully, is conflicted. This seeing of the "self", without condition, enables wisdom to enter. Self honesty requires that we challenge everything that we were ever taught, everything that we've ever thought to be true. Self honesty also requires that we challenge our experiences. Often times, our experiences are seen selfishly, and not truthfully, thus we often times miss the wisdom that existed in those moments. Through self honesty, we can no longer assume anything, everything must be seen through honest eyes. Everything must be challenged to ensure that it is rooted in peace, Love, and freedom. And what does not exist within peace, Love, and freedom, must be dissolved within us. What is truly sacred can only be seen through Love, peace, and freedom. Love, peace, and freedom are all interchangeable. One cannot exist without the other. When one is present, all are present. When one is not present, none are present. This is the beauty of life, this is the beauty of you. This is the truth of us, that must be seen.. honestly.

BEYOND THOUGHT #6
THE DISSOLVING OF FRUSTRATION

Frustration is often times seen as inevitable. Many of us have accepted this to be a part of life. Some of us attempt to move beyond it by suppressing it. But very few have truly dissolved frustration in their lives. The dissolving of frustration is very possible within one's life. It does require self honesty though. To truly see frustration as it is, one must be willing to explore it totally as it arises. Frustration is simply the movement of expectation not being met repeatedly. This happens when we selfishly desire something, and it doesn't happen the way we desire it to happen, when we want it to happen. Initially, the feeling is disappointment. But over time, it becomes the movement of frustration. When we are frustrated, we are no longer capable of peace. Which means we are also no longer capable of being Loving, or free. The thoughts that exist when are frustrated are thoughts of frustration. Thoughts rooted in frustration are not peaceful at all. Our thoughts, when we are frustrated, carry hurt, resentment, suppression, even anger. This is why we must be willing to face frustration honestly. When we are willing to face it honestly, and see the hurt it brings to us, we can then move towards dissolving it within us. Since self honesty is rooted in self Love, we can use self honesty to see the hurts of being frustrated in a highly sensitive way. We can also self honesty to see that the hurts of frustration are of our own doings. We can then discover that frustration only exists when we are not willing to honestly accept the fact of a given situation as the truth of it. Once we discover this truth, we can then see the traps of frustration. One trap that leads to frustration is selfishness. When we are selfish, we are very capable of being frustrated easily. Therefore, we must be selfless to move beyond frustration. When we are selfless, we are then capable of seeing things in a selfless way. This allows the beauty of the truth to genuine present itself to us. When we are selfless, we are no longer blind to the truth objectively. However, when we are selfish, we are blind to everything truly beautiful. Through selfishness, we only see what we want to see selfishly. Selfishness destroys everything beautiful within a genuine moment. Frustration removes the beautiful opportunity for wisdom. When we are frustrated, we are short sited, narrow minded in thought, and very selfish within our feelings. While frustration provides energy, it's energy is no good in terms of healing. This is why Love never truly comes from frustration. So if frustration is to ever be dissolved, one must be willing to see life honestly, selflessly, and without fear.. to ensure that Love remains through life's challenges.

BEYOND THOUGHT #7
THE UNDERSTANDING OF TIME

Time has been approached in many ways, by many different people from many different backgrounds. Time, in one sense, is very necessary. Then, in another sense, is extremely disruptive. Time exists in two ways. One existence of time is physical time. The other existence of time is psychological time. While physical time is real, psychological time is a total illusion. Physical time is the time we use to describe walking from the kitchen to the bedroom, or learning a new language. In these cases, it will take physical time. It would be impossible to instantly go from the kitchen to the bedroom, or to go from only speaking one language to two languages fluently without time being present. However, we have taken this same truth of physical time and adopted it psychologically. This is where the disruption and distortion begins. With psychological time, we often say that it will take time for us to cool down when we are upset. But is this really true? Or, are we just conditioned to using time this way for our own selfish purposes. For example, not many people would say "give me a second to get happy, I'm working on it, just give mean some time." But we use these same statements adversely, when it comes to us moving from one emotion of choice selfishly, to another of desire without honesty. Here is another example: One person is angry, by choice of course, then they attempt to move away from anger without self honesty. Because the desire of anger hasn't been seen honestly, the anger remains selfishly, until that person gets tired of feeling that way, or is ready to dissolve the anger and choose a different emotion. This process is purely psychological in terms of time. These statements imply time selfishly, and are only used when we are not interested in true, honest change; "I'm working on it, I'm getting better at it, It's gonna take me some time to change my ways, I can't just change overnight". The truth of the matter, is that it actually doesn't take "time" at all to move from one emotion to another. For example, if you are in a pleasant, somewhat peaceful mood, and someone screams at you aggressively, it won't take any time at all for your mood to change. This ability to change moods goes both ways. If you are upset, and you see it honestly through peace, it will dissolve within you instantly. You will see the hurt in it, and instantly move away from it. Not in a way to escape it do to fear, but because you truly see the hurt in being that way honestly. It would be similar to you realizing the water is hot, and moving your hand away from it. You don't move your hand because you are trying to escape it. You move your hand because you actually understand the harm it can cause you. You can then stand and watch the water as it runs hot, without fearing it. You can then observe it fully, watching the steam rise from it as it touches the cooler air. This is the wisdom that comes from understanding time. Time, in itself, is beautiful when understood. It provides us with intelligent decision making abilities in the physical world. It also allows us to express ourselves creatively in the physical world. When time is understood, truth and wisdom remain available. But when time is not understood, it becomes fear, and it becomes everything but the beautiful truths of life.

PERSONAL ENTRY #23 – 10:42PM
A NOTE TO SELF

I cannot be discouraged. I must not be discouraged. Nothing I do can be done out of fear, or out of haste due to time. I must understand the traps in living such a life. I must understand that no soul on this beautiful Earth deserves me that way. As the true beauty of my life must exist in theirs also. I must continue to live without fear, share my heart openly without the need for approval. I must do so because it is the very thing that makes me alive. I must do so because it's the truth of me. I must do so because you are worth living for. This note to self, must not be used as a reminder, but as the truth of me within this moment. This note to self must not be seen as a stepping stone towards greater enlightenment, but as the truth of me within this moment. Because if this note to self is seen as anything other than the truth of me in this moment, I would have totally missed the beauty of my life.. in this moment.

PERSONAL ENTRY #24 – 2:13AM
WE ARE MEANT TO "BE"

I often explore life with you, without even knowing who you are physically. It's the genuine playfulness of creativity blended compassionately with the seriousness of truth. I've discovered what is necessary to Love you. I've gifted my life to it. There is no hesitation in exploring my emotions this way. I remain sensitive to my changing ways to ensure that Love is a constant. I've grown so much for you. Just to say this brings a smile to my face. I'm far from a hopeless romantic, I would consider myself to be quite different than that actually. I would call myself a hopeful realist. See.. the beauty of hope provides the opportunity for genuine vitality without expectation, and the realist accepts the truth of any situation without bias. So with this carefully placed combination of truth and desire, whether I meet you are not, we will forever be meant to be.

PERSONAL ENTRY #25 – 7:16PM
NAÏVE, NOT AT ALL

To put it simply, I don't turn a blind eye to anything. I'm very aware of my surroundings. At one time, I was the surroundings. The understanding of Love hasn't turned me into a man that runs from adversity or discomfort, but a man that embraces it totally. As the beauty of true growth happens most in times of challenge. I face my life honestly, every step of the way, and what a beautiful discovery it is. I accept truth wherever I see it, I run from it never. I feel the full movement of my emotions as they arise and dissolve daily within my life. So the pure in-joyment that you see within me, isn't because of any lack of awareness in terms of what's going on, but because I'm totally aware of what is going on around me.. and within me. And what's within me is peace, because I totally accept the truth of the world, and myself.. enough to not become the hurts of the world.

PERSONAL ENTRY #26 – 7:01AM
PEACE "IN" QUIET

It's quiet here, just the cars occasionally humming outside my window. My thoughts and desires are beginning to meet my senses this morning. I'm just getting this day started. The quiet here is peaceful, there is no disruption in it at all. I am also peaceful, no disruption within me at all. I am totally still within my mind. Although desire is arising and my senses are awakening, there are quietly doing so within me. They are not disrupting the peace within me at all. They are not removing me from the quiet that exists outside of me this morning. It's a beautiful feeling to just "be".. quiet. Not quiet by simply not speaking, but quiet within your spirit. This feeling is very humbling. In this moment, I realize just how selfless Love is, as this quietness allows me to observe the world without any need for ego. I am here amongst life, while life is living. I am observing it all quietly, and peacefully. In this moment, I also realize the wisdom found in selfless observation. I see the needs of others, in place.. and out of place. It's as if I'm just standing by without being visible. My senses are heightened to these subtleties, because my desires are not overriding the truths of life. This peace this morning does not come without change, it just comes without the disruption of everything that is truthfully.. "quiet".

PERSONAL ENTRY #27 – 12:27AM
THROUGH YOUR WINDOW

Your heart is beyond precious. To feel you would be a desire met peacefully, in the purest way. Not to feel you physically, but to feel the life of you, through your heart. To truly exist within the passions you place close to you. To deeply understand why your soul responds to desire the way it does.. intimately and honestly. This is the window I seek to see through, your window. Life's meanings can be discovered through your window. Your eyes represent the physical site of your soul to me. To see your eyes, with my soul.. would be everything to me. Just to see your heart, your spirit, your existence.. through your window.

PERSONAL ENTRY #28 – 2:59PM
BEFORE I KNEW YOUR NAME

"Deeply, without pressure, without the need for intellectual understanding, I desire to move towards you. You being everything and nothing, you being what is, what was, and what may be. The possibility of you fills me beyond consciousness. It's as if I was made for you and.. there is no way at all for me to avoid you through honesty. You don't have a face, or a name. You are more than just some random feeling to me. You are life, itself. From as early as I can remember, I wanted to understand you. I wanted to learn all about you. It seems as if many don't truly understand you. I say this because I would ask about you all the time. It's almost like you are somewhat of a myth. I hope to meet you one day. I hope to be close to you one day. So close, that others will not be able to tell us apart from one another." ..Those words, were the words of my heart before I knew your name. ..Now I call you.. "Love".

PERSONAL ENTRY #29 – 12:54AM
ETERNITY

It's as if time stands still when I'm with you. The way in which conversation flows without any forced effort, brings life to me. When we speak, it's as if we are exploring our thoughts and feelings together in unison. I didn't realize I desired so many things in the same ways as you do. I didn't realize so much growth could be discovered in genuine, honest communication. It's as if we are traveling through lifetimes when we speak. The honesty you share shows me that you truly care about your life. I gladly mirror this sentiment with you. The way you take your time to truly explain what it is that you feel, shows me that your attentiveness to yourself, in life, is extremely important. I mirror this sentiment also. Maybe we are exploring eternity together. Eternity being everything sacred, maybe we are sacred "together". Maybe we are changing the world together. Maybe others could even join us. Maybe the beauty of eternity.. is truly meant to exist for all of us.

PERSONAL ENTRY #30 – 10:54PM
FROM JUDGMENT TO ACCEPTANCE

Earlier in my life, it was very difficult for me to move away from judgment. I knew that I didn't want to judge. But the reason why I didn't want to judge was simply because everyone "else" had told me that it was wrong to do. At that time, I didn't truly see the hurt in judgment, because the people that were telling me not to judge were still judging others. They were even judging me. So, being young and influential, the contradiction I saw in those I looked up to brought about confusion within me. I began judging myself in a very critical way. I would end up dealing with moments of depression because of this self judgment. If I got a bad grade in class or dealt with any form of rejection, it would actually hurt me emotionally. I would attempt to suppress it, and on the surface I became very good at it. Not many people truly knew what I was going through internally. However, during this time in my life, I learned a very valuable lesson. The lesson I learned was that there is a very fine line between caring and not caring. When you care improperly, it's very easy to become destructive within your own life. It's also very easy to lose sight of caring altogether. Because we are able to care, we are able to feel things. This care brings with it passion. So when we care improperly, meaning when we care in a selfish way, the energy of passion is very hurtful, very selfish. Love and true wisdom cannot be found in care when we are using it selfishly. When we care improperly, or selfishly, we make ourselves the center of everything. We are not able to truly care for others when we care improperly, because we can't even truly see them. We must explore and use the qualities of care peacefully, or we will inevitably hurt ourselves, and those around us. Many people come to us for truth. If we are selfish, we cannot share any truth with them in a genuine way. We can only provide them with opinion when we care selfishly. There is no beauty in opinion. There is no Love in opinion. Opinions have created war. However, there is great beauty and Love in truth. As a child, I received a lot of opinions, not many truths. This led to many years of confusion for me. This led to improper relationships. This led to many years of self inflicted heartache. All the time, I was not "purposefully" hurting myself or being hurtful to others, I just hadn't yet figured out where I was going wrong. This is a feeling I began to grow tired of. I began to no longer want to be in unhealthy relationships, I began to no longer be okay with just going through life being unhealthy within myself emotionally. I began to truly see the change that would be necessary for peace, compassion, Love, and sincerity to be restored. I would have to totally accept my life, and the lives around me.. peacefully. I could no longer judge myself or others. I could no longer get upset with the way someone else desired to live their own life. I could no longer beat myself up emotionally if I fell short of a goal. These changes, through acceptance and the honest observation of my actions through peace, have offered me great wisdom. Every day is now an opportunity for healing and growth, instead of more hurt. Every moment in my life is now an opportunity for wisdom, and not confusion. Every experience in my life is now felt with a genuine sense of openness. So now.. it's impossible for me to judge you.. because I've learned to genuinely accept you just the way you are.

PERSONAL ENTRY #31 – 11:25AM UNTIL NOW

Thoughts are taking shape in my mind. The places they hold are ordered. They are becoming plans. These plans don't represent the truth of anything though, as plans are subject to change fairly quickly in actual life. They are simply thoughts put together through my desires. Easily, these thoughts could control me if I'm not careful. These thoughts could lead me to acting and pursuing my desires improperly, because they are thoughts. What we "think", is never the actual truth of anything. The truth is what exists whether we "think" of it or not. For example, if I don't think of the tree outside, that doesn't make it not "be" outside. This is true because I can actually "see" the tree outside without "thinking" of it. This, in itself, humbles me daily. This truth allows me to appreciate the beauty of not thinking and just "be-ing" in my life. I say this because I understand deeply that what I "think" is simply the gift of imagination. The gift of imagination that I must use peacefully and properly to keep dreams from turning into nightmares. Thought and truth can however exist peacefully together. We just have to understand that thought has nothing to do with it... "now".

PERSONAL ENTRY #32 – 5:25PM
WHAT IF

What if all of our actions were genuine in life. What if actions were not rooted in fear. What if we accepted the truth of everything. What if we kissed only when Love was present. What if we truly desired to be good to one another. What if we did good things for ourselves and others regardless of where we thought it would get us in life. What if we didn't divide ourselves with nationalities, color, gender, and sexual preference. What if we did not judge at all. What if I Loved you unconditionally, from the beginning. What if you Loved me unconditionally, from the beginning. What if we never intentionally tried to hurt each other. What if sex was sacred. What if intimacy was explored honestly. What if life was this way.. for you and I. What if life was this way.. for all of us. What if..

PERSONAL ENTRY #33 – 6:43AM
HAVE YOU HEALED

Frustration no longer eats away at me. I'm no longer disrupted internally by the opinions of others. Everything is just everything. I move through my life honestly. Accepting what I'm good at, as well as what I still must work on. There is no bias within me. If something is factual, I accept it immediately regardless of where it comes from. As the fact is still fact. I live a fairly simple life now, simplified because the complexities of selfishness, hurt, peace, compassion and Love are understood. I've taken the time to heal myself. I've taken the time to heal myself by Loving myself. There will always be enough time in the day for this activity of self Love to exist within me. I make certain of it. Emotional maturity is deeply understood. I now understand "fully", that I am my emotions. This understanding is rooted in a genuine sense of inner-peace, so deeply that I no longer accept the emotional hurt of others as my own. This is truly a beautiful way to live. It enables me to remain beautiful for you. It enables me to compassionately do what I can.. to help someone else heal.

PERSONAL ENTRY #34 – 9:27PM
OUR CREATION

Kisses are beautiful when sacred. No lust, just the pure action of affection brought forth through the genuine feeling of honesty and compassion that arises within Love's intimacy. Touch also becomes amazing, when it's pure. It provides the senses with a way to communicate without bounds externally. It is very possible for this "real" feeling to exist within us together. We just have to be willing to "be".. within "it". I cannot meet you without Love unconditionally, if I truly desire to "be" with you in a deeply pure way. I cannot be willing to exist falsely in any way with you. I must be willing to truly "share" my life with you peacefully and passionately. If we both meet each this way, we then have the ability to create the beauty of newness for one another. Every moment we share, thereafter, will be pure and sacred for the both of us. Nothing we touch will become tainted. No kiss will ever exist without Love's beauty.. and no one will ever be able to destroy what we have created.. ever.

BEYOND THOUGHT ENTRY #8
A GENUINE REQUEST

A genuine request comes from a very humble place. This type of request often leads to beautiful conversation, and /or a beautiful relationship. This type of request sustains the availability of Love, peace, and respect between two people. This type of request also allows the opportunity for dialogue to exist freely. For example, a genuine request is a request presented without expectation. It's a request made with sincerity. It's a request made with the willingness to accept any and every response peacefully. When this type of request is present, it comes with peace, it comes with Love, it comes with sincerity. There is nothing within a genuine request that is selfish. Someone capable of a genuine request, is incapable of argument. If you attempt to argue with someone that has just made a genuine request, they will not respond hurtfully. They will accept your response peacefully, as the truth of your response provides them with the honesty they were seeking from their request. Although genuine requests are beautiful in nature, we have to be mindful of the requests that are not genuine. These requests are rooted in selfishness. They seek a certain, particular answer or response. They do not exist freely without bias. They are often times rooted in judgment. This type of request can become a demand very easily. For example, I can ask you to go to the store with me, but when you say "no", I can get upset and begin to treat you differently. This happens because my request was not genuine. If my request was genuine, I could have still asked you to go to the store with me, but when you said "no", I would have been okay with it. Without treating you differently, without getting upset, while still accepting the truth of you peacefully. A genuine request does not mean that I lie to myself with how I'm feeling after your response. It doesn't mean that I suppress my feelings to make certain that you can't tell what I'm feeling. It just means that I can't blame you for what I may be feeling. When my request is genuine, I must honestly look into myself to discover the root of my feelings. I must also understand that my feelings are determined by the value I placed on your response. I must never stop Loving you based on your response. However, I must maintain Love for myself in the process of Loving you. So if your response to a genuine request requires me to leave you in order to Love myself, I must leave. Not in a way to stop Loving you, but in a way to ensure that peace and honesty remains within me, so that Love remains in a way that enables me to continue to Love myself enough to Love you. When a request is genuine, it is not presented in a way to remove freedom from anyone. It's actually presented to ensure that freedom is not removed at all. As Love is freedom, a genuine request must also carry the quality of freedom. This is why a genuine request cannot be rooted in an expected or specifically preferred response. When this is understood, what we ask of others, remains beautifully pure.

PERSONAL ENTRY #35 – 6:56AM
SOLITUDE

It's never the same. This feeling of being alone is beautifully serene. I grow immensely when I'm alone. The stillness around me removes the distortions of life. I am now able to truly discover who I am and who I've been, without the concern of who I may become. This solitude is a place of healing for me. Love exists unconditionally here. It is a place where I'm able to challenge my feelings honestly, to ensure their place and purpose in my life. I need this time alone. This time alone leaves me with no escape from the full responsibility of what I feel. The beauty I find in being alone, frees me from the ills of insecurity and attachment. This enables me to exist with the wisdom needed to be alone.. without being lonely.

PERSONAL ENTRY #36 – 9:06PM
FATIGUE

Today has been challenging, beautifully so. The honesty of who I am, and where I am.. is very present. I appreciate the truths of me. The acceptance of the truth of me allows me to respond truthfully within myself. This self honesty is beautiful, even in challenging moments, because it brings with it the quality and wisdom of self Love. Physical fatigue is the truth of me in this moment. Physical fatigue rises within me mainly when I don't rest properly, and I must say, lately I haven't been resting properly. However, physical fatigue is something I no longer fight with. It has become something I truly accept as my body's way of telling me to rest. I listen. I've been staying up late and getting up early for several days now. This process has caused me to now be forced to rest. When this happens, I know it's not by accident. I typically do this when I seek to meet goals I set for myself. These goals are not static, but milestones that are able to be moved. I never set anything in stone, because I never know the future. This allows me to accomplish things in my life in a very natural way, without pressure or disappointment. This also allows me to remain mentally capable of caring for myself properly. For me, physical fatigue enters before mental fatigue. The hurt I see, is becoming mentally fatigued due to physical "self created" circumstances. If I'm not mentally available to you, I must not be physically available to you. This ensures that I exist properly, not just for myself, but for you also. Because unconditional Love requires that I not only think of myself, but the existing world around me.. as well.

PERSONAL ENTRY #37 – 4:57PM THE PURSUIT OF DESIRE

Between nothing and everything, silence and total chaos, we exist. We have always existed this way. As for as I can remember, I have always existed this way. It's interesting how we never truly get used to the same things happening over and over again. It's as if repetition isn't a natural state of "being" at all. It's interesting how we always desire something different, even in the most subtle of ways. This desire can exist in freedom, or it can exist in control. Between nothing and chaos, and between silence and everything, desire can be placed at any point. This placing of desire is ultimately our doing. No one forces us to place it in peace or conflict. We make this decision based on how we see life, how we live life, who we care about in life, and who we don't care about in life. But what is fundamentally true within all of us, is this desire to not repeat the same day over and over again. This becomes disruptive within us because we are not robots. It becomes disruptive because the truth of life is a moving, tangible, explorative, thing. When desire is pursued without freedom, peace does not exist in the desire. This can lead to anything from a slight disruption within oneself, to the total destruction of oneself altogether. Desire pursued through freedom comes with it's own intelligence. True freedom makes it possible for desire to not be disruptive. This is because freedom is rooted in Love as well as peace. So where there is freedom with desire, the desire can be explored totally and peacefully within oneself. This pursuit of desire through freedom can also lead to anything from a subtle healing to occur within oneself to the total healing within oneself altogether. This is the beauty of desire, this is the beauty of Love, through desire.. this is what makes desire pure.

PERSONAL ENTRY #38 – 6:37AM
WAKING UP

I often wake up without even thinking about myself, but of others. It's almost as if I run through a responsibility checklist at times, to make sure everything else is in order before thinking of myself. I do this because I rarely go to sleep thinking of myself. By the time I'm to rest, I've already moved past any concern I could have come across during that day. I don't carry issues with me at all. I deal with them when they arise as best I possibly can, then leave them there. When I sleep, for the most part, it's a very comfortable experience. My mind is clear, gratitude is my mood, and I've already prepared myself for the possibility of tomorrow's beautiful truths. So this is why I often times wake up for you. It's not because I get some sense of entitlement or boost egotistically from it, but because I'm already taken care of within myself. My work for myself was done the night before. So when I wake up, I'm now available for you internally, mentally, physically, compassionately, and Lovingly. I must say, it feels good to wake up this way. It's the discernment that comes from understanding that we are all here together. It's the clarity that comes from not placing my problems or issues on anyone else. It's the wisdom that says, "rest your soul". It allows me to maintain peace from night to day. With me, there is no wrong side of the bed, just the beauty of waking up to you. Just the beauty of being present.. "for" you.

PERSONAL ENTRY #39 – 5:49PM
PEACE TO THE PUZZLE

There is no human existence without the existence of another. I cannot exist without you. Man needs Woman, just as Woman needs Man. This is the truth of us. Over the many years, we have begun to attempt to alter this truth. However, what is sacred in truth, cannot be altered. Scientifically and physically it doesn't take a Man and a Woman to create a child anymore. But naturally, it does. This is not to say that there is something wrong with science. However this does bring up the question of whether or not we are applying science properly. This is where the distortion and separation begins. We must understand deeply that what is natural, is pure. What is natural, exists within the freedom of Love. What is natural, also brings with it wisdom. Nothing constructed through thought can be done in the name of Love. It's the pure action beyond the boundaries of thought, where Love actually exists. This separation from truth is happening due to selfishness and incorrect teachings. Selfishness creates emotional hurt, and emotional hurt leads to deeper selfishness and emotional hurt. It's a very vicious cycle that cannot cure or heal itself. It just continues to become more and more selfish, more and more hurtful, until it destroys itself. This is what many of us are doing in the world. We are hurt, so we are hurting others, and we are hurting ourselves. Which also implies that we are selfish, and becoming more and more selfish, which in turn separates us even further from what is beautiful natural within us. Life is natural, Love is natural, peace is natural. So when we live without peace and Love, it should be no mystery as to why we aren't happy internally.

PERSONAL ENTRY #40 – 8:33PM
THE EXISTENCE OF YOU

Nothing in life must be taken for granted. Gratitude makes room for affection. A peaceful spirit brightens life's colors. From one day to the next, your passion must be to simply explore. Explore everything that is you, everything that changes your mind, and everything that touches your heart. It's what you are here for. Wisdom has the ability to be communicated through you. Life favors you, this way. Your experiences are forever your own here. The uniqueness of your existence will never be duplicated. You are naturally a gift to be Loved, a vessel to be cared for, and a soul to be cherished. So much is provided to you each day to ensure your existence. So much is required for every moment of your life to remain real. The balance of life on this planet accepts you graciously. Oxygen, the Sun, the sounds, and the beautiful things in life that make your existence real, are all here to exist "with" you. So don't ask what is there to live for, ask what is there not to live for.

PERSONAL ENTRY #41 – 2:05AM CHALLENGES

It is in the most challenging time of your life, that you have the opportunity to grow the most. It is also in this time, when you face the greatest danger of your spirit breaking. This time becomes an opportunity to grow, or to shrink. If you shrink, this moment in your life will return again someday to challenge you again, and again, and again. If you grow through it, this moment in your life will never show itself as another obstacle ever again. To truly grow through such a moment, you must be willing to face every fear it presents. You must be willing to Love "through" it. As Love will be your way to gain the wisdom needed to dissolve the internal disruptions and hurts such a challenge could cause. When we are faced with these challenges, it's because we still have areas in our lives that haven't yet been addressed completely and honestly. This is life's way of showing us what areas we still need to work on. Don't run from this challenge though, be willing to accept the honesty of it. In these moments, the truths of us are revealed whether we are ready or not. If we are not ready, there is a chance we will shrink in this moment. However, if we are ready, we will find enormous growth in facing our truths. Through the discovery and "facing" of the truths within us, wisdom becomes our path. This genuine discernment is brought through honesty. It's the pure quality of self honesty, in a peaceful way, that brings with it Love's actions. So again, don't run from the challenge, because within that challenge is Love.. just waiting for you to grow.

PERSONAL ENTRY #42 – 11:41PM
I'M WITH YOU

Not sure where you are in life, but just know that I'm with you. My life does not exist without caring for yours. We fundamentally need the same things, so I must go through life with you. The difficulties in life, we share. Your challenge is my challenge. My compassion is available to you. With great respect and carefulness, my actions are thought through to ensure that they are not hurtful towards you. Before I go to sleep, I make certain that my heart has room for you. Peace is my offer, understanding is what you will receive, and Love will forever be unconditional.. from me.. to you.

EXPERIENCES #1
BEAUTIFUL BEFORE

She was born a beautiful little girl, filled with life and vitality in a genuinely pure way. Her innocence was infectious, and the clarity of her smile was beyond measure. She was willing to explore life fully, because she was "born" this way. No hurt, no ill emotion towards anyone, just naturally.. beautiful. But then, the hurts of the world came to meet her. Confused, because no one around her had truly prepared her for life through Love's understandings, she became affected. So even though she existed innocently and beautifully, she was able to be hurt by others. Her innocence was a born gift, but she was never taught the beauty of unconditional Love. So the hurtful ways of the world began to hurt her. Little by little, her beauty began to fade. Her heart grew sore, and less available for healing. She began to distance herself from her explorative nature, because she would often encounter more hurt because of it. Her explorative nature, however, was the "truth" of her. It was what she was truly here to do. So within her, she died even more. She hadn't given up on Love, she just had no way of finding it within herself. External methods to heal, only seemed temporary. She would soon find herself in that same place of hurt, all over again. This was a process of attempting to escape hurt, that she would encounter for many years to no avail. Now she's an adult, still that beautiful little girl deep down inside, but because she's hurting.. she's no longer able to feel the genuine beauties of the world.

This is the experience of not just the Women of the world that are hurting internally, but the Men of the world as well. We are "all" born beautiful.. many of us have just misplaced our beauty.. along the way.

–Love Heals..

EXPERIENCES #2
THEY WANTED TO BE MEN

They wanted to be Men, but they didn't exactly know what it meant to be Men. They were raised in broken homes. Some broken physically, in a way where they were only raised by one parent. Other homes were broken internally, meaning both parents were present, but unconditional Love was not present. Structurally these boys grew up differently, but fundamentally they all grew up the same. In the physically broken home, they lived with one parent that struggled internally. The single parent did their best, but the single parent also felt the pressures of providing for these young Men. The single parent would have moments of mental and physical exhaustion, because all of the weight was on them. This would sometimes lead to the unintentional neglect of the emotional needs of the young Men. This emotional neglect, also existed in the internally broken homes. Although both parents were present for these young Men, there was no pure emotional continuity within the family. The Mother and the Father attempted to get along, but because they were not fundamentally together for the "right" reasons.. they conflicted. These conflicted moments didn't always happen in front of the young Men, but they could tell when their parents weren't pleased with one another. The energy in the home was different, and they noticed. The parents had different fundamental ideals in terms of life. These fundamental differences led to the disharmony and lack of unity when it came to raising these young Men. The Mother would say that one thing was okay, and the Father would say that it was not okay. Conversely, there were times when the Father would say that one thing was okay, only to have the Mother disagree. All the while, these influential young Men were being introduced to confusion by their parents unintentionally. Instead of learning how to Love, these young Men were actually learning how to live "without" Love. This experience, for them, had the same emotionally affect as it did for the young Men in the single parent home. And because all of these boys learned how to live without Love, they became Men that didn't truly know how to appreciate Love. They became Men that didn't genuinely see unconditional Love as necessary anymore. They desired Love as boys, just as they desired to be Men, as boys. But they had developed and learned a life so far from Love, that they no longer thought that unconditional Love was truly possible.. with someone else.

This is the experience of not just the young Men of the world that experience a childhood without Love, but of the young Women in this world as well. We are "all" born with the desire to Love.. many of us have just given up.. along the way.

–Love Heals..

PERSONAL ENTRY #43 – 4:50PM
WOULD YOU MIND

I could speak to your heart indefinitely. I could exist with your life beyond time. I could even explore the fullness of my life with you.. but would you mind? Deeply in-tuned with life, I know I need you. The harmony we owe the world, waits for us. The purest of our desires are in Love's presence.. just waiting for our souls to touch. It seems as if forever isn't long enough, but that's only when I see you through the eyes of time. So through the purest vision within my heart, I ask for your hand in eternity.. would you mind?

PERSONAL ENTRY #44 – 1:43PM
GOOD

What feels good to me, is the honesty of you. The acceptance of your life, your spirit, your desires, and your imperfections.. make life beautiful to me. It would be totally disrespectful for me to place my eyes upon you falsely. It would also be totally irresponsible for me to only meet you.. halfway. You deserve all of me, the fullness of my capacity in terms of Love, the genuine entirety of my soul's existence, and the eternity of peace that only my actions can show are true for you. I must meet you this way, I must exist with you this way, because this is the only way you can truly feel good.. to me.

BEYOND THOUGHT ENTRY #9
PAST, FUTURE, AND REAL

I never really look back. I have my moments, but I don't stay in the past very long. I seem to only reflect when necessary. I wasn't always this way, but it seems as if I've naturally grown into "being" this way. I now reach into the past only to improve the present. I do this because I know that what's in the past has already been done. So for me to go into the past now, it must be the movement of me exploring memory in a way to help me move forward in the present. Because the beauty of the present requires that we remain in the present, we have to be careful when we go into the past. There are many traps set psychologically in the past. For example, one psychological trap that I used to fall into, was the trap of past experiences. Often times, if we have a bad experience or even a good experience, we seek to duplicate that experience or move away from that experience in the present, without even giving the present a true opportunity to be "real". A bad experience in the past, for example, could lead to our creativity being limited. While a good experience, in the past, could possibly lead to us negating our own safety. There are many traps in the past, just as there are many traps in the future. So we must be willing to stay in the present as often as possible, because only the present is real.

BEYOND THOUGHT ENTRY #10
ACCOMPLISHMENT

Accomplishments are beautiful, but don't stop and admire them so easily. Since the feeling of accomplishment is totally psychological and temporary, it has a tendency to wear off and give way to stagnancy. The seeking of accomplishment can also have us pursuing it improperly. This is the danger of superficially being a goal chaser. Because when we pursue goals beyond peaceful principals, we are pursuing them selfishly. And when we pursue goals selfishly, they have the ability to become hurtful to ourselves, and to those around us. They even have the ability to cause us to never reach any of the goals that may follow. Therefore, before setting a goal, we must fully understand it's value and purpose in our lives. We must explore it through honest questioning. Will this goal add to my life in a way that will allow me to add to the lives of others? Will this goal be the best way for me to reach my "end goal"? Questions like the two just stated, keep our focus within the pure principals of life. This way, if the pursuing of the goal ever shifts away from these principals, then we know we are pursuing the goal improperly. All principals must be rooted in peace, Love, and compassion, or else we will just be constructing something new that further hurts the world.

BEYOND THOUGHT ENTRY #11 NIGHTMARES

Nightmares are the result of unresolved fears. It's the movement of the subconscious mind as we sleep. When we rest, the conscious mind also rests. The subconscious mind then takes over. So what has not been resolved consciously, slips into our subconscious as we rest. This happens because the mind seeks security. When the mind is insecure, it will continue to work through an issue until it finds security.. even if it has to find a "false" sense of security. This is why we must be careful with the information we take in. Often times, information is being processed by our minds without us even knowing it. This can be very dangerous when we are unaware. However, once we truly heal ourselves from the hurts of the world, information no longer controls us. This movement is the freeing of the mind through genuine awareness. This is also the only way to truly exist without the distortion of lies. So in order to remove nightmares, we have to remove the lies that bring about psychological fear. To truly understand what brings fear, we first must understand the movement of thought itself. Thought, being the movement of memory, can manifest itself in the mind many different ways. To ensure that thought occupies the proper place in the mind, we must be secure. Psychological security requires that we not use imagination to distort the present moment. It also requires that we accept everything as it actually is "now".. not in the future, not in the past, but actually as it is right "now". When we truly "do" this, fear has no room to be present, because thought is no longer being used to manipulate the truth through our imagination. So when we go to sleep, without imagination distorting our present, we then go to sleep with clarity. The facts remains the facts. No distortion, no fear, no lies. All is accepted and accounted for actually, without worry. Because worrying is nothing more than imagination playing with the future in our present.. and the truth of the future, is that it never comes. The future remains the future, just as the past always remains the past. The only truth is "now". So when we understand this deeply, the subconscious no longer has to work through the information that hasn't been processed properly during the day. It can then take on the regular functions, which are to truly allow the mind, body, and spirit to rest.

PERSONAL ENTRY #45 – 9:41PM
GROUNDED

I don't do things in life for anyone's approval. I do things simply because they are the right things to do. By "right" I mean peaceful, just, genuine, and Loving. I've learned that by sharing my actions this way, I will never hurt anyone intentionally. Therefore, if someone was hurt unintentionally by my actions, I cold then genuinely apologize to them and grow from my mistakes truthfully. I live this way because I'm serious about my life, seriously peaceful within my life, seriously Loving within my life, enough to seriously care about you.. and your life.

PERSONAL ENTRY #46 – 12:56AM
INNER PEACE, IT WASN'T EASY

I've had to heal myself from all of my hurts. Hurts that initially I didn't even realize I had caused. Some hurts I didn't even realize existed within me, until I began to see myself honestly. It wasn't easy. A lot of my relationships changed. Some people I began to talk to less, and some people I began to talk to more. It wasn't an immediate thing, it was a gradual thing. As I changed, the things I was interested in doing and talking about started to change. I began to no longer relate to them the way I used to. I began to be interested in seriously deep discussions regarding the way the mind worked. I wanted my actions to be pure, so I no longer wanted to lie to myself and I no longer wanted to hurt anyone. This led to me being alone a lot of times. This also allowed me to truly see the beauty in being alone. I realized in aloneness, I was honest. I also realized that within honesty, there was peace. This peace, within me, seemed to dissolve my hurts. In peace, I had no desire to be hurtful to anyone. The notion of hurt didn't even enter my mind when I was peaceful. This feeling made me never want to move away from peace again.. and this was the beginning of my true journey.. of "never" moving away from peace again.

PERSONAL ENTRY #47 – 9:05PM
A RELATIONSHIP

I want to relate to you the way Love relates to peace. I want us to be deeply connected in a way so fundamental, that no "one" or no "thing" could cause disruption within us or between us. I want the smell of your scent to feel like home to me. Honesty available, I want to share all of the beautiful emotional truths with you. Freedom available, I want to explore every desire you keep close to you in the most genuinely unconditional way. Love available, I would use eternity's creativity to uniquely show you beyond measure, that this relationship will forever be sacredly real.

PERSONAL ENTRY #48 – 6:19AM
HUMBLED

The feeling when you first wake up is the most beautiful. Your mind is transitioning, your body is rising, and your heart is open. Everything within that first moment of waking up is instinctual. It's the miracle of life itself. I'm grateful to be blessed with such a miracle. I'm humbled every morning of my life by it. I would thoroughly enjoy sharing this moment, every morning of my life, with a lady that appreciates this miracle just as much as I do.

PERSONAL ENTRY #49 – 2:36AM
I SEE YOU, INTERNALLY

It's so beautiful the way I see you. I don't see your flaws at all, just the truths of you. You have a certain way about yourself that's uniquely your own. It has everything to do with how beautiful your heart is, mixed with everything the world attempts to put in your way. It's also extremely beautiful, the way I feel you. Not physically at all, but deeply.. intrinsically. I carry the same gift as you. The world has also put many obstacles in front of me. So when I say I see you, it's because I see myself in you. The gratitude for your life has become instinctual. My soul only wants the best for you, because my soul desires to truly "be".. with you.

BEYOND THOUGHT #12
RELATIONSHIP: THE PURSUIT OF SECURITY THROUGH INSECURTY

Just about all of us desire to be with someone. Just about all of us would agree that life is better when we are in a Loving relationship. A Loving relationship for us, brings with it so much growth and beauty. It adds to life immensely. The world changes once we become truly Loving with another. So why is it that we have such a problem coexisting together in a Loving way with someone? Is it because we are not totally secure within ourselves, meaning we deal with personal uncertainty in a way that brings forth fear or the feeling of being inadequate? Or, is it the fear of not being able to truly "be" ourselves with someone else? It's actually both, as well as all other aspects of life rooted in insecurity, fear, and expectation. Most relationships these days are "trade offs". A relationship that's a trade off, is a relationship that does not exist with freedom, therefore insecure. When we are in a relationship that is a trade-off, we are emotionally and physically confined. We are also enslaved to the expectations of our partner and our partner is enslaved to our expectations. This is how a trade off works.. if you meet my expectations, I'll continue to meet yours. The moment you stop meeting my expectations, which may very well be you finally becoming honest within yourself, I'll stop meeting yours, which may very well be what was honestly within me also. There is no "truth" in such a relationship, just as there is no genuine honesty within such a relationship. There is also no real freedom within such a relationship, and where there is no truth, honesty, or freedom, there can be no Love or Peace. Where there is no Love and peace, there is no security. So when we pursue relationships without Love and peace, we inevitably pursue them in an insecure away. Insecurity will never bring security. And this insecure approach to relationship, is what has continued to keep us from truly feeling the beauty of unconditional Love with another soul.

PERSONAL ENTRY #50 – 10:52AM
CHANGING

I'm changing.. every day. In every moment I'm changing. I no longer have expectations for these changes, I just change. I no longer move away from changing when it brings peace, I embrace it. The fact is, that none of us truly ,stay the same. We either change in ways that bring peace, or ways the further increase conflict. Some of us may feel as if we are set in our ways, but even in those ways, we are still changing. Subtle modifications are still happening within us, based on our desires and emotions as we go through live. So the truth is, as long as we are living, we will change. This is the truth of all of us. Change is, in fact, inevitable. The fact that change is truly inevitable, was something I didn't really understand when I was younger. I was never educated in the pure movement of change as it related to peace. Therefore, before I truly understood Love as peace, I would often fight change. There were many times in my life, where the need for me to change could not even be realized. It was as if I was totally blind within myself in certain instances. There were also many times when I saw the change that I needed to make, but I selfishly just didn't want to. This confused, unloving, immature, irresponsible way of living disrupted my life for many years. All of these changes that I needed to make, were being blocked simply because I was too hurt to see that they were truly necessary for my personal healing. Instead of changing, I would validate my "lack of changing" by concerning myself with the amount of "time" or "effort" that I had invested into a particular thing or situation. I would use time and effort as a way to justify not changing. This internal fighting went on in my life until I truly realized that change, itself, was not the problem. The problem was my misunderstanding of change. See.. the whole time I wasn't changing, life actually was. Change itself is beautiful, it implies life, because what is truly living.. actually changes. So with me fighting change, in essence, I was no longer "living". For me to live, truly live.. I would have to change, but I would have to change peacefully. This understanding of the necessity of peaceful change, changed my life forever. I no longer fight change, because I no longer fight life. And because I no longer fight life, I no longer fight the truth as peace.. within myself.

PERSONAL ENTRY #51 – 7:18AM
EMPATHY

I'm a peaceful man, but the disruptions of life do not go unnoticed. There are horrors that exist in the world. Many of these hurtful human acts exist daily. They range from a simple "no", out of selfishness, to the actual killing of another human being. I see these things in life, and I feel them deeply. I feel them deeply enough to make certain that my intentions have absolutely no relation to what they represent. The desire of peace is where I place my heart and my actions. However, the responsibility of peace is honesty. So for me to truly be honest with myself and to you, I must not overlook or belittle any act of hurt in the world. I must also ensure that there is no blockage that exists, as I observed that hurt. As human beings, we are taught and conditioned to see life selfishly. This selfish conditioning creates a blockage between the truth and us. This blockage is then able to create a distortion, which keeps us from truly seeing the significance of hurt in another person, as the hurt that exists for all of humanity. For example, if I am rich and not properly educated through peace and selflessness, I may not truly see or feel the effects that exist within the life of someone that is poor. I may not be a bad person, but I may find it very easy to overlook their pain simply because it's not directly happening to me. This would be a blockage. This would separate me from that person empathetically, and where there is no true empathy there can be no genuine concern. Just as where there is no genuine concern, the energy needed to uplift someone, dissolve a problem, or selflessly see the truth, cannot exist. I have learned and accepted this truth as my way of life. Within me there are no longer any blockages. My heart, my spirit, and my life are open to see and feel it all. So with everything within me, I do my absolute best in an extremely serious way, to make sure that my actions are Loving. Because if you are hurting, I will see it and feel it empathetically, and the hurt that may exist within you, must be met with the Love, care, and compassion that exists within me.. always.

PERSONAL ENTRY #52 – 6:57PM
REAL

I'm very capable of saying a lot of things that "sound" good. I can even put words together in a seemingly beautiful, imaginative, creative way. But if these words that "sound" good to your ears and eyes, are not rooted in genuine truth to ensure that it remains good for your soul as well, then all I'm doing is lying to you, and there is absolutely nothing deeply beautiful, intrinsically imaginative, or internally creative in a lie. Therefore, I won't these writings "creative" at all.. I'll just call them truthful.. I'll just call them "real".

PERSONAL ENTRY #53 – 1:03PM
SUPERFICIAL

Why are we superficial at all? What genuine benefit to life exists within superficiality? If no one was superficial, what would the world look like? Would jealousy exist? Would there be war? Would make-up be necessary? What would beauty truly mean? These are some of the questions I ask myself, as I explore the movement of superficiality. I don't explore superficiality with a preconceived outcome. I don't start my exploration of it with the determination of whether or not it is bad or good. I simply look at the movements of it without bias. If we were to explore superficiality, we would see that it is rooted in insecurity. We would also see that it requires validation and cannot exist without measurement or judgment. It has no way of encompassing Love because it has no way to see Love. So if it has no way of seeing Love, what good comes with being superficial? If good implies peaceful, then there can be no true goodness born of superficiality. Superficiality blocks genuine communication. Superficiality also blinds us to true beauty. So, if we are to truly Love someone, we must not pursue life with them in any superficial way. The instant we see them superficially, Love is no longer present. Now, after exploring superficiality this way, we must at least, ask ourselves this "one" question. Am I superficial? For me.. the answer is no.

PERSONAL ENTRY #54 – 4:59PM SELF LEARNING

Our attention is the truth of us. Where we place our attention says so much about who we are as human beings. We often forget this human truth because in the moments of genuine attention, we forget that we even exist. In pure attention, we become one with where our attention is placed. Our attention is rooted in many things. To begin to understand attention, we must see that our desires, values, needs, and environment all play a part in where our attention goes. So to truly see yourself honestly, you may find it helpful to start by observing what you place your attention on.. and why you place your attention on it.

PERSONAL ENTRY #55 – 6:01AM
BETTER

Every opportunity I get, I seek to improve. Even if I don't succeed, my intent was still to improve. I live this way because of the responsibility I've placed on my life as a human being for you. Although it's a responsibility that comes with great value, it doesn't feel cumbersome to me at all. I learned a while ago, that if any particular way of living feels difficult to you, it's only because you haven't become it yet. For example, if your way of living involves conflict, you will find it very difficult to live peacefully.. until you become peaceful. But if your intended way of living is already peaceful, you will have no difficulty at all if asked to attempt to live life peacefully. It would be no real struggle of difficulty to you. Adjustments may have to be made, but you would make them willingly. So when the honesty of you is in line with the way you desire to live, the movement of improvement becomes you as well. It will begin to happen naturally in the form of discipline, you will begin to grow "in that area" as you go through life. Learning, changing, and the effort it takes to do so will no longer wear you down. Instead, it will become the very thing that drives you.

PERSONAL ENTRY #56 – 7:10PM
THROUGH PEACE

Through peace, I'll go to the moon and back with you. Through peace, we can explore the entirety of life together beautifully. Through peace, I will forever be attracted to you. Through peace, I can't help but to Love you. Through peace, we were born to be together. Through peace, life with you would be genuinely fruitful and compassionately easy. Through peace, we would never share the movements of hurt with one another. Through peace, we would only exist to Love one another. Through peace, we could grow together beyond measure. Through peace, we can make all of this real. Through peace, I'm now asking you to exist with me. So through peace, please say you will..

PERSONAL ENTRY #57 – 4:03PM
YOUR LIGHT

Underneath it all, I know you mean well. Life has just been extremely difficult and seemingly unfair. I must also say that you're not alone in this feeling. I feel this feeling "with" you and "for" you as well. If only so many of the things that have happened to you, could've gone differently. Maybe the hurt your beautiful heart carries would not be so burdensome. Maybe some days wouldn't seem so dark. I know exactly what you feel, because I feel this "with" you and "for" you also. If life would just compassionately kiss you for a change, the good it would do for you would be immeasurable. I know this also, because I deeply understand your heart, and I feel it "with" you and "for" you. If tears start to fall from those beautiful windows of your soul, please don't stop them. Water is simply removing the hurts. Your eyes are helping you heal. The wetness on your face is Love. The darkest days are over. The emotional feelings you now experience, will only exist to represent the movement of you becoming your own light.. and I know this.. because the light that is within you is also the light that is within me.. so what you feel, I will forever feel.. "with" you.. and "for" you.

PERSONAL ENTRY #58 – 8:32PM
BAGGAGE

If it doesn't add to you, you must not "add" it to you. If it slows you down or hurts you in any way, you owe it to yourself to move away from it as peacefully and as quickly as you humanly can. Life, for all of us physically, is a finite thing. However, the finite truth of life must not create anxiety or haste. But instead, may it bring with it a beautiful seriousness to your life, that promotes Love and genuine growth internally. Whenever we hold on to things that don't add to us, they weigh us down. They slow our growth and block many of life's blessings. Unfortunately, many of us may feel we understand this, but still hold on to them anyway. This happens because we are not truly ready to let them go. Often times, fear is the reason. Fear, being totally illusory, often keeps us from having the proper capacity to try something new, even if we know we must. This fear is rooted in inadequacy. It causes us to feel as if we will fail if we pursue a different reality for ourselves. This irrational way of thinking keeps a lot of people in hurtful relationships, jobs they particularly don't care for, and from genuinely pursuing their desires fully. Living this way also leaves room for regret, and regret disrupts the energy of gratitude within us. Without gratitude, the energy needed for self exploration and self Love is stunted. Without gratitude, we are also not capable of receiving the meaningful blessings of wisdom that come through sincere humility. This carrying of baggage, and not being able to let it go, is the main reason many beautiful hearts still exist with hurt today. Heal yourself.. by letting.. it.. go..

PERSONAL ENTRY #59 – 11:32AM
IT'S YOU AGAIN (LIFE)

They just don't see how beautiful you are. I can't help but think about you. I've even tried to move my attention to something else today, but it keeps coming back to you. You are everything I stand for, as I exist with a soul that will not become ill. You are so beautiful to Love, you are so beautiful to me. So many people in this world exist with you inside of them. It touches me deeply to know I'm not the only one that understands and feels your presence. And the beauty of you, is that you exist within us the whole time, just waiting for us to internally accept you. The story of experience and wisdom, maybe you will be a later book for me. But until then, I thank you for gaining my attention today. May you continue to move to the front of my mind and heart whenever necessary. I'm grateful for you just as my maturity appreciates you. So with you being life, there is no way for me to exist genuinely without Loving you. Personally.. I know you are not the problem.. it's us..

PERSONAL ENTRY #60 – 1:14AM
TRANSITIONS

As a child, I liked you. That childlike innocent kind of liking, free from many of the ills I would later have to endure. It was as close as I could possibly get to Loving you. I would think about you in a joyful way, expecting to see you, wanting to be with you. You were the experience of everything new to me. I was child, not yet a mature Man, not even a young Man, so the innocence showed in my shyness towards you. I would learn from you. Your life was quite different from mine, and I found that interesting. I also wanted to learn more from you. I was not in competition with you, because I hadn't yet been corrupted with society's definitions of gender roles and classism. It was as if we knew our places within each other's lives. Then, I grew a little bit older. I still liked you, but this was a different kind of liking. I was not yet a mature Man, but I was old enough to socially take care of myself. Due to societal conditions and my personal lack of wisdom, what was once an innocent "liking" as a child, had now become infatuation. My desire was different this time, I still wanted to learn from you, but now I wanted you in a way that would also meet my personal needs. My desires, I would now see in you. I would not see them in a way to personally hurt you at all, but I would see them without that genuine sense of care required for me to Love you. I was affected by society, very influential and naïve to life's truths, I would say that I Loved you without even understanding what it truly meant. But I meant well, I just didn't know how to purely show that through my actions. The shyness was gone, the transition from shyness became apprehension. I went from inquisitive as a child, to cautious as a young Man. Now I am a mature Man. The liking, as a child or as a young Man, no longer has a place in my life when it comes to the matters of the heart. Love has dissolved the movements of them both within my actions beautifully. I can now truly Love you, not simply "like" you. I can now be emotionally available to you peacefully, without the confusions of infatuation, desire, or lust. Now the innocence of truly desiring to learn from you, has returned. The innocence of meeting you as equal to me, has also been genuinely restored. I can now see you without the falsities taught through society. I can now see you without life's hurts. I am now capable of seeing you purely, as the beautiful soul that you truly are. So now, being that I'm a mature Man, I can no longer carry the hurtful ways I had as a young Man.. or a child ever again.. because now.. I Love you..

20153178R00056

Made in the USA
San Bernardino, CA
30 March 2015